Let's see. . . About Me

A WORKBOOK OF FUN WAYS TO LEARN ABOUT YOURSELF

The Center for Applied Psychology, Inc.
King of Prussia, Pennsylvania

LET'S SEE. . . ABOUT ME: A Workbook of Fun Ways to Learn About Yourself
by Hennie M. Shore
Illustrated by Steve Barr

Published by:
The Center for Applied Psychology, Inc.
P.O. Box 61587, King of Prussia, PA 19406 U.S.A.
Tel. 1-800-962-1141

The Center for Applied Psychology, Inc. is the publisher of Childswork/Childsplay, a catalog of products for mental health professionals, teachers, and parents who wish to help children with their social and emotional growth.

Printed in the United States of America.

ISBN 1-882732-46-4

CONTENTS

INTRODUCTION

Let's See About Me is a workbook of exercises to help children develop a positive self-concept. The book is divided into four sections corresponding to the A,B,C's of helping children: Affect, Behavior, Cognition, and Social System. These are the basic building blocks of a child's personality and also correspond to the basic modes in which children can be taught to look at themselves and their problems.

The first section deals with emotions. These activities are designed to help children understand their basic emotions as well as the feelings of others.

The second section deals with behavioral issues that are important to children including following rules, dealing with anger, and understanding the consequences of one's behaviors.

The third section of the book includes activities that teach children the relationship between their thoughts and their behaviors. These activities help children learn to have a positive attitude, to plan ahead, and to problem-solve.

The book concludes with a section on a child's social relationships with his or her family, peers, and community.

Using this book. . .

This workbook was primarily intended for use by counselors and teachers to help individuals or groups of children learn about themselves. Each activity is designed to give children new ways to think about themselves and others, and to reinforce this information by writing and drawing. The exercises can also be read by an adult to groups of children and then used as the basis for discussion.

SECTION I: UNDERSTANDING EMOTIONS

All feelings are okay—it's what we do with them that's important.

Understanding and controlling one's feelings plays an important part in learning to get along with others. There are many different kinds of feelings, and we all have each one of them at different times. Sometimes we can even feel two or three different feelings at one time.

Understanding the emotions of others is also important, because it affects the way people feel about others. If you are sensitive to the feelings of others, they will like probably like you. If you're not, they'll probably do what they can to avoid being with you.

1. Anger

Everyone feels angry sometimes. It's only natural. In fact, it's good to feel anger sometimes, and it's good to express your anger instead of keeping it all bottled up inside you. Releasing your anger in constructive ways almost always helps you feel better, and less angry.

Name three things that make you angry.

1. If I have to dring orang juice.
2. If I dont get my own way
3. If I want something I can't have

But some kids seem to be angry all the time. Sometimes, we say that a person has a "chip on his shoulder," which means he always looks like he is ready to fight.

Why do you think that someone would be angry almost all of the time?

Because there mom and dad were to poor to get them anything they want,

There are a lot of things that you can do when you are angry. Some are helpful, but some are not.

Can you think of three good ways to express anger and three ways that expressing anger would not be helpful?

Three good ways to express anger:

1. Count to ten.
2. take deep breaths
3. do childs pose

Three ways that people express anger that are not helpful:

1. Stopping you feet
2. Shouting
3. ~~Mak~~ making growing noises,

Draw a picture of something that would make you angry.

Draw a picture of something that would take away that anger.

2. Sadness

Sadness is an emotion that people try to avoid. But this isn't always possible. Humans feel many emotions, sometimes ones we don't like. That is part of our "make-up."

These are situations that make people sad:

When someone dies.
When someone is sick.
When you miss someone.

Can you think of a situation where you were very sad?

___

___

___

Ask three people what makes them sad. Write their responses below:

1. ___

2. ___

3. ___

Sadness is only a problem when it lasts a long time. Even if people have a reason to be sad, they must learn to accept whatever happened and go on and enjoy life.

Peter was sad because he moved to another city. He missed his friends, he missed his old room, he missed his grandma and grandpa. What would you say to him that might make him feel better about his new life?

___

___

3. Fear

Everyone is afraid of something. Some people are afraid of a lot of things. Some people are afraid of things that they don't really need to be afraid of. Sometimes it's called "fear of the unknown."

List five things that children should be afraid of:

1. very big things
2. monsters
3. ghosts
4. witches
5. vampires

These are some common things that children are sometimes afraid of, but they needn't be. What would you say to children who are afraid of these things?

The dark "Its okay just pretend there is a light on"

Bugs "I know they are creepy but you should thin how scared they are of you!"

Thunder and lightning "Don't worry it would not hurt you"

Getting a fatal disease "Its okay, think of all the kids who are too poor to get a doctor."

Mark was afraid to walk past the old house on the corner. No one had lived in the house for many years, and it looked really scary with its paint peeling, shutters falling off, windows boarded up, and the tall grass littered with trash.

Do you think Mark was right to be scared? Why or why not?

Yes and No. Why because it looks so creepy and something evil could be living in the house.

No beca its probaly just old

What could he say to himself that would make him feel better?

"Its halloween, its only decorations."

What would you say to him?

"Its okay, just go quickly by the house".

Sarah's parents fought all the time. They walked around angry all the time and wouldn't talk to her very much. She was afraid they would get divorced and no one would take care of her. Do you think she was right to think that she would be abandoned? Why or why not?

No I do not think she will be abandoned because her parents love her very much, and are just very angry at each other and are to mad to talk to her.

Do you think she was right to think that her parents might get divorced? Why or why not?

Yes I think she was right that her parents might get divorced because it might mean that they just do not love each other any more because they are fighting.

What could she do to make herself feel less scared?

Hang out with her friends more if she can.

Describe a scary situation that happened to you.

I was worrying that I would See Julia and Isabel at the pool and they are not my friends anymore.

What could Colby do to feel less scared?

4. Being Happy

Everyone wants to be happy all of the time, but that is not possible. Kids have problems, just like adults, and they have to learn to solve them and sometimes accept them.

When people are unhappy, they sometimes have to work at finding a way to be more happy. This seems like a strange idea to some people, because they think that happiness should just come naturally, like on some TV programs where everything always works out by the end of the show. But that isn't the way things work in real life.

already happend in your life.

What are some things you do to cheer yourself up when you are unhappy?

1. Think about good things that

2. do yoga

3. tell your mom that you

are that unhappy

name three

~~What one~~ thing would ~~you~~ change about your life to make yourself happier?

1. Make more new friends

2. play more

3. Be kinder.

Draw a picture of yourself, surrounded by things and/or people that make you happy.

5. Understanding Others

An important part of getting along in the world has to do with understanding how other people feel or see a situation. When you have a real understanding of how another person feels, it is called "empathy." Understanding another person's point of view is important in problem-solving and relationships.

What does this expression mean: "You have to walk a mile in another person's shoes to understand him?"

What have you done that made your parents really mad at you?

Do you think that they had a right to be mad? Why or why not?

Allan was furious at his mother. She didn't have time to help him study for his test, and he failed it. She was late picking him up for school. Now they were in the grocery store, and she was talking to a friend, while he needed to change for baseball practice. He was about to explode!

What would you do in this situation?

How do you control your temper when you really have to?

Brian was ashamed a lot of the time because he stuttered. He hated to talk in public, but when he was called on in class, he had no choice. What do you think his teacher could have done to help him feel better about himself?

Susie was always sad because her father was very sick and was going to die. Everyone felt badly for her, but that didn't make her feel any better. What do you think Susie could have done to help herself deal with these feelings?

What could other people have done to help Susie feel better?

SECTION II: BEHAVIOR

It's important to have good behavior in order to get along with other people. People tend to like children who behave well, and even though it's sometimes fun to misbehave, kids who know the limits and consequences of bad behavior are better liked and more socially secure. This helps them feel good about themselves.

6. The Importance of Rules

These are some rules that are usually important in a household:

Never touch a hot stove.
Always keep the front door closed.
Turn out the lights when you leave a room.

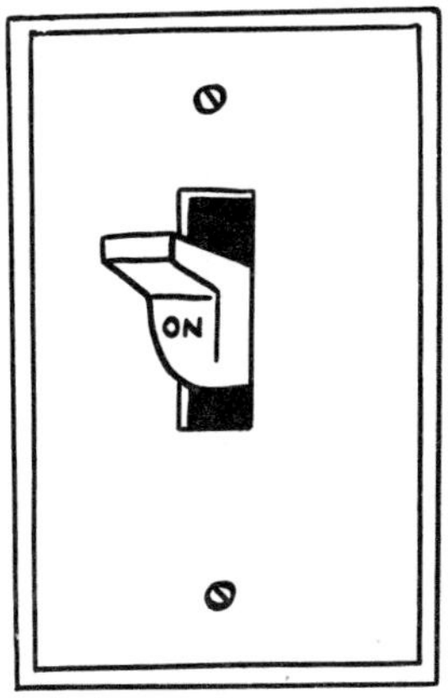

Clean up!

What are three important rules in your house?

1. After plating with a game

2. ______________________________

3. ______________________________

List three rules that you think aren't so important.

1. ______________________________

2. ______________________________

3. ______________________________

Draw a picture of yourself following a rule at home.

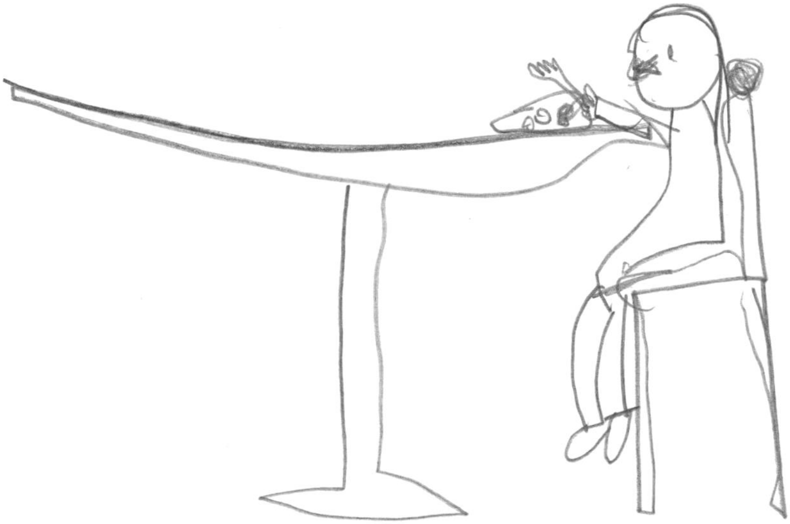

What are three important rules in your classroom?

1. ______________________________

2. ______________________________

3. ______________________________

What could happen if there were no rules in the classroom?

____

____

____

Draw a picture of somebody breaking a classroom rule.

What would happen if nobody paid attention to the teacher?

7. Aggression

People usually don't like kids who are aggressive. You probably know a few—they're the kids who fight when they're angry, push you out of line in the lunchroom, and generally do exactly what they want to do even if it means hurting someone in the process. They're the kids who get in trouble with the teacher often. They're the kids other kids try to avoid.

Do you think it's ever okay to be aggressive? If so, give an example.

Some parents use spanking as a punishment for aggression. Do you think that children should be spanked when they are bad? Why or why not?

Why might a grown-up who was spanked as a child do the same to his own children?

Pretend somebody hit you. Write down the first words that come into your mind.

What do these words tell you about how you feel about being hit?

If someone hit you, what would you do about it?

Is it ever okay to hit back? Why or why not?

8. Anti-Social Behavior

Most people don't want to be with people who are anti-social. When someone's anti-social it means that he/she does things that would annoy or bother most people, like:

Ignoring them when they say "hello."
Pushing to be the first in line.
Not sharing his/her snack with someone who forgot to bring one.

Suppose you were the Judge at Kid's Court. Who would you put on trial?

What did he/she do?

What kind of punishment would you give him/her if he was guilty?

Draw a picture of someone doing something for which he/she should be punished.

Do you think that jail helps criminals become better people? Why or why not?

What might be a better solution to get criminals to change their ways?

In some countries, government officials cut off a person's hand when he steals and cut out his tongue when he lies. Do you think that this is right? Why or why not?

Why do people join gangs?

Do you think gangs are good or bad? Why?

How is a gang different from a group of friends who hang out together?

Ricky was a boy who didn't seem to like anybody. He kept to himself. He always looked angry. He never seemed to need anyone. What do you think made him act this way?

What do you think would make him change?

Amy was a girl who bullied everyone who crossed her path. She didn't have any friends. She teased other kids, made fun of them, and generally harassed them until they would do everything to avoid her. Why do you think she did this?

What could you say to her to get her to change?

9. Study Habits

Some people think that they can get good grades, or grades that are good enough to pass a subject, even if they don't study at all. Sometimes this works. But these people are fooling themselves—they're not learning anything, and people who don't learn new things and expand their minds turn out to be dull and failures in society.

Can you think of three reasons why it is important to study and get ahead?

1. ______________________________

2. ______________________________

3. ______________________________

Taylor liked nothing better than to get away with stuff in class. He pulled the hair of the girl who sat in front of him, shot spitballs at the other kids and never did his homework or studied for tests. He spent a good part of each day in the principal's office. Why do you think his behavior was so bad?

____

____

____

What do you think made him act this way?

____

____

____

What do you think of kids who act this way—do you think they're cool, or not cool at all?

Every night Bobbie's mom would ask her if she'd done her homework, and Bobbie always said "yes." But what Bobbie was really doing was talking on the phone with her friends and watching TV. Her grades were terrible, but she didn't care. Why do you think Bobbie didn't study?

Do you think she was right or wrong to try to get away with this?

What should her mother have done to make sure she was telling the truth?

____

____

____

What could her teacher do to help her be more aware of the importance of doing her school work?

____

____

____

10. Self-Reliance

It feels really good when you rely on yourself. It makes you feel powerful, and confident that whatever you decide to do will be okay. It makes you feel independent, too, and you know that you are responsible for your own actions.

Marty was the team's star player. He liked the attention he got by being the best, but sometimes he felt like he had the "weight of the world" on his shoulders—being best made him feel really pressured to excel. He would get really nervous before each game, and it didn't feel like "fun" to him.

What could he have said to himself to relax?

What could he have said to his coach and teammates so that he didn't have to feel like everyone else relied on him so much?

Have you ever been a team "leader?" What did it feel like to you?

Draw a picture of yourself as team leader.

Draw a picture of people working to do something together, as a team.

Greg was beginning to get nervous about the three tests he had to study for—they were all on the same day! How would he ever learn it all? How would he ever keep everything straight in his head? He had good study habits, and he planned to study a lot, but this was scary.

What could Greg say to himself to get "perspective?"

____

____

____

How could he calm himself down?

What would you do if you were in this situation?

11. Self-Motivation

Self-motivation refers to giving yourself an extra "push" to do something that you might not really want to do. It strengthens you and gives you the incentive to do more, and it helps you feel more confident and self-assured.

As do most kids, Chris wished the summer would never end. But Chris had another reason for dreading summer's end—he was starting a new school and he didn't know anyone who went there.

What could Chris do ahead of time to help ease his way into his new school?

____

____

____

List three things that you could say to Chris to make him feel less anxious.

1. ____

2. ____

3. ____

Tell about a time when you felt nervous or anxious about something.

____

____

____

Draw a picture of Chris on his first day at school.

Draw a picture of a situation in which you felt anxious.

12. Being Independent

Sometimes people are forced to decide whether or not to go along with the crowd, or with their best friend, or with anyone else who wants them to do something they're not sure they want to do. People who feel "secure" in what they want know that if they follow their own instincts things will turn out all right. It's called being independent.

Independent people are happier in general than people who depend on others for satisfaction and contentment, and they usually get what they want and accomplish what they set out to do.

An independent person might:
Go to see a movie by herself.
Join a club in which she doesn't know anyone else.
Buy a gift for his mother's birthday without consulting anyone else.

Can you think of three more examples?

1. ____

2. ____

3. ____

Sally's best friend Carrie wanted to sign up for after-school sports, and she wanted Sally to join up with her. Sally wanted to join the after-school Girl Scout troop that met on the same day, and really didn't care if Carrie joined up with her or not. In fact, she thought it might be nice to make some new friends.

Do you think Sally was right to do what she wanted to do? Why or why not?

____

____

____

Would you go along with your friend just because she or he wanted you to?
Why or why not?

____

____

____

Draw a picture of a new group you'd like to join.

Being independent also involves motivating yourself. Sometimes people have to "push" themselves to do something they might feel nervous about or afraid of doing. Most people who do push themselves end up feeling very proud of themselves, and it gets easier for them to do such things each time they accomplish them.

Keith knew that if he didn't try to make friends at camp, he'd have a terrible summer. But he was so nervous! Taking a deep breath, he asked Jake and Nick to shoot some hoops with him. Soon the boys were planning to sit together at lunch.

Why was it so important to Keith to make friends?

Do you think Jake and Nick admired Keith's self-motivation? Why or why not?

How do you think Keith felt when he thought about how brave he'd been?

Tell about a time when you were self-motivated.

Kelly's grades never got any better even though she studied hard for every test. She was beginning to think that she was just plain dumb. She wanted to get good grades, but it was so hard!

What could Kelly tell herself to help her continue to try?

____

____

____

What would you say to her to help her motivate herself?

____

____

____

Could her teacher help her in any way?

____

____

____

13. Assertiveness

Most people think about asserting themselves after something happens that makes them angry. They think, "Why didn't I speak up for myself?" Sometimes it's hard to ask another person to see their point of view. They're afraid that if they assert themselves, other people won't like them as much. But they're wrong. Usually, people who are assertive (without being aggressive or offensive) are better liked and respected, and they like themselves better too.

Chuck didn't like being teased for wearing a tie to school every day. He liked wearing ties, and he was determined to dress the way he wanted to dress. He thought, "Why should anyone else care? It's not hurting anybody. It's none of their business," but it was hard for him to actually say this out loud.

What could Chuck have done to assert himself?

Why do you think the other kids picked on him?

Why do you think people feel threatened when someone else does something in a different way?

Draw a picture of someone doing something to assert himself.

Tyrone was sick and tired of having to do all the chores around the house just because his brother was always practicing his part for the school play. It wasn't fair!

What could Tyrone do to assert himself?

Do you agree that it wasn't fair for Tyrone to do all the chores? Why or why not?

Tell about a time when you asserted yourself.

Tell about a time when you should have asserted yourself.

14. The Awareness of Rules

Some kids think grown-ups make rules just to keep them from having fun. But rules are important because they offer a way to control things so that everything and everyone doesn't get "out of control." People who know the rules and follow them get along better with others and in the world in general.

Eddie and Eric were playing on the school playground after school. Eddie suggested they try to break into the equipment shed to get a basketball. Even though Eric tried to talk him out of it, Eddie broke the lock and got the ball.

Do you think Eddie was right to do what he did?

____

____

____

Do you think Eric could have done more to stop Eddie from doing what he did?

____

____

____

What would you do in this situation? What would you say to Eddie, if anything?

____

____

____

Talia's dad told her she could get a hamster for her birthday, but that she had to be responsible about feeding and caring for it. Talia promised she would, but soon after she got her pet she lost interest in it and didn't care for it at all.

What do you think happened?

Do you think Talia should be punished for her behavior? Why or why not?

What do you think is a good punishment for Talia's behavior?

Why is it so important to be responsible in situations such as this one?

Have you ever broken an important rule? Tell about it.

15. Taking Responsibility for One's Actions

Sometimes a person does something wrong and she has to take responsibility for it. For instance, if you decided to paint your room hot pink without telling your mother first, you'd have to take responsibility for your action. If you got grounded for a week with no TV, that would be the consequences of taking responsibility for your actions. Hopefully, you'd learn a lesson, and you'd never do anything like that again!

When Talia's hamster died because she didn't take care of it, her dad told her that since she hadn't cared for the hamster, she would have to take charge of deciding what to do with it, and then follow through with her plans. He called this "taking responsibility for her actions."

Do you think Talia's dad was right to do this?

What could Talia say to her dad to convince him to give her another chance to be responsible?

Tell about a time when you had to take responsibility for your actions.

Danny never cleaned his room, no matter how many times his parents tried to get him to do it. When he borrowed his friend's best baseball card, he forgot to return it, and a dish of melted ice cream spilled all over the card when he slam-dunked his shirt onto his bureau. His friend told Danny that the card was worth $25.00, and that he expected him to pay for it.

Do you think it was fair for the friend to expect Danny to pay for the card?

____

____

____

Did Danny do anything wrong in this situation? What did he do?

____

____

____

What do you think Danny should do so that something like this doesn't happen again?

____

____

____

16. Understanding the Consequences of Behavior

Most people know that if they behave in a way that is unacceptable, they will have to suffer the consequences (be punished, etc.). They understand the consequences of bad behavior, so they try not to behave badly. People who do behave badly must understand what the consequences of their behavior will be, and most of the time when they "suffer" the consequences they learn a lesson so that the bad behavior doesn't repeat itself.

Andy teased Billy's cat all the time, and the more Billy reacted, the more he did it. His mother told him that each time he teased the cat, he'd get a "strike," and when he had three strikes, he'd be "out." "Out" meant that he'd lose a privilege, like no dessert or no TV for that evening. Sure enough, this wasn't enough to get Andy to stop teasing, and soon he found himself with nothing to do because he couldn't watch TV.

Do you understand the consequences of Andy's behavior? What were they?

Were they fair?

Write about a time when you had to "suffer" the consequences of your behavior.

Letitia didn't know why her mother wouldn't let her eat all of her Halloween candy in one evening. She snuck up to her room and began eating, starting with her favorites, of course. She woke up in the middle of the night feeling REALLY sick. Now she understood why her mom told her to save some candy for each day.

Why is it a good rule to portion out Halloween candy?

____

____

____

Why is it a good idea to listen to your parents?

____

____

____

Draw Letitia with her candy on Halloween the next year.

What is she doing with her candy?

17. The Right Behavior at the Right Time

Most people know how to act and react at any given time. If you fall and cut yourself, your parent's reaction would be to take care of your cut and help you feel better. If you hit a home run, your parent's reaction would be to give you a big "thumbs up" (and probably a hug too). Their reactions trigger the proper behavior at the right time.

Robert's mom was feeling very sad. His dad had told Robert that his mom was "depressed." Robert felt very bad, and wanted to make his mom feel better. He wasn't sure what to do, but in the meantime he gave his mom a big hug.

Do you think Robert was right to do this?

Do you think it made his mom feel better or worse?

Do you think it helped Robert feel better?

How have you helped someone feel better?

Draw a picture of your experience.

Arlo's mom was sad and upset when she and Arlo's dad got divorced. Arlo began to help her do things around the house, and soon he was doing a lot of the stuff his dad used to do when he lived there. He felt good because he was helping his mother, but he was tired all the time and didn't have much chance to play with his friends or even to do his homework.

Do you think Arlo was right to "take over" for his dad?

___

___

___

Why do you think Arlo thought he should help his mom so much?

Was it right for his mom to expect him to do so much?

Was there ever a time when you did something that you thought shouldn't be your responsibility?

Draw someone acting in a responsible manner.

SECTION III: COGNITION

People with high self-esteem have developed a way of thinking about themselves and the world which focuses on the positive instead of the negative. This means that they think good thoughts about themselves and they have an "inner-voice" that makes them be able to do things that might take a little more effort than other things. They are able to decide things for themselves (without the help and advice of others), and when they make decisions, they feel good about them. All these cognitive skills help people behave in ways that make them happier in the long run.

18. Believing Things That Aren't True

Some children, usually those with low self-esteem, think things about themselves that aren't true. For instance, a person can think that she's too fat even though she weighs 20 pounds less than she should. She thinks that people would like her better if she were thinner. She might even know "intellectually" that this isn't true, but "emotionally" she believes it. It's a "false belief," even though it's real for her.

Joanna knows that it's not cool to take drugs, but she thinks no one will like her if she doesn't join the others. To her, there's no choice—she has to do it to be cool.

Do you agree?

I do not agree with her.

What could Joanna tell herself to make it okay in her own mind not to take drugs?

I think she should say drugs are bad for me in her head to remind her not to take them.

What could she say to the other kids when they tell her she's not cool if she doesn't join them?

She could say if you want to do that you may but I don't want some one to tell me what to do, and I don't want to get sick.

Tell about a time when you were expected to do something to fit in. Did you do it? Why or why not?

I don't remember doing sothing to fit in.

Adam's parents are at their wit's end with him, but he couldn't care less about what they think. He and his friends have punk haircuts, dyed green. They've pierced their noses and they wear only black clothing. Adam thinks he's cool, and it doesn't matter what his parents or anyone else thinks.

What do you think?

I think it is not a good choose to do this becaue I think you should act who you are and so people can see how you are yourself.

Why do you think some people try to look different?

I think they try to act diffrent and lot of other things.

Draw a picture of someone who's doing something to be cool.

Give some examples of things people do that they think is cool but that other people do not.

1. D~~Y~~YE There hair

2. act different

3. pierce there nose and other places.

19. Modifying Behavior from Within

Have you ever seen someone talking to himself? People talk to themselves all the time to cheer themselves up, to make themselves try harder, and to concentrate. Athletes even say that if they can imagine themselves running faster or jumping higher, then they actually perform better. In these ways they are modifying their behaviors from within.

Richie was always doing things to embarrass himself, like making stupid faces and noises in class, and spilling his lunch all over his shirts, and tripping over his feet in the hall. The more he did these things, the more he got teased. At first he tried not to do them, but eventually he just told himself, "Maybe I really am a geek. I can't help it."

Is there anything he could have told himself to stop this behavior?

Don't try being a jerk.

Have you ever had trouble stopping yourself from doing something that you knew would get you in trouble or teased? Write a few lines about it.

I Don't Know

How did it feel?

Why do you think this happens?

Liane decided once and for all that she was going on a diet and sticking to it. She was tired of all the kids making fun of her because she was fat. She had a salad for lunch, but later that day, as she was about to pass the ice cream store, she thought, "Oh, one more ice cream sundae won't matter." What could Liane have told herself to help her walk past the ice cream store?

Its only a junk yard.

Why do people have trouble listening to their inner voices?

I am not sure!

Why do people have trouble ignoring their inner voices?

Because they realry want to do that thing.

Why do you think people tease others?

Because they are

diffrent than them, thats

what they could think

20. Planning Ahead/Weighing Alternatives

Planning ahead takes forethought, or thinking about the consequences of something before it happens. If you plan ahead and prepare for an event, the likelihood of the event running smoothly is much greater than if you do things on the spur of the moment.

Weighing the alternatives refers to sorting out the options, or choices that you have, and then deciding which is the best for the situation.

Judy knew three weeks ahead of time that her history report was due on the 20th. She didn't take the time to prepare for it, though, and when she realized that it was due the next day, she knew she was in trouble. She didn't even have the books to use for her research.

What should Judy have done?

____

____

____

What are some ways to plan ahead?

1. ____

2. ____

3. ____

Have you ever forgotten to plan ahead? What happened?

____

____

____

Pam's mother asked her to visit her grandmother on the way home from school. Barrie asked Pam to come over to study with her after school. Pam knew she needed to study, but she also knew her mom would be angry if she didn't visit Grandmom. What are Pam's alternatives?

Is there any way Pam could visit her grandmother and study with Barrie?

How would you solve Pam's predicament?

Make a schedule for the day for Pam to follow.

21. Developing Age-Appropriate Insight

Insight is the ability to "know" how something will turn out before it actually happens. Although it is impossible to really "know" this, people who have insight feel that something will happen in a certain way, and they act accordingly. "Age-appropriate" insight refers to how developed a person's insight should be at various times in their lives.

Tommy couldn't find his baseball glove. He dumped everything out of his drawers and closet and still didn't find it. He thought, "Mom will understand. She'll put all this stuff back while I go out and buy a new glove with the money she gives me."

Do you think Tommy's insight into how his mom would react was right?

What do you think would really happen?

What should Tommy have done in the first place when he couldn't find his glove?

Mary felt that no one liked her, but she was mean to everyone, sat by herself at lunch and never smiled. She felt that the kids in her school were the meanest in the whole world. Do you think she was right to think this?

How should she have changed her behavior?

Do you know anyone like Mary? Write a few lines about him/her.

22. Problem-Solving

When you solve a problem, you are actually fixing something that wasn't quite right by using your ability to think things through and work out the best solution for them.

Mario was having a lot of trouble understanding the teacher. She'd stand at the blackboard and spout out instructions and facts and figures, and he couldn't keep up with her. He began to daydream, and soon class was over. He told himself, "Boy, I'm glad I made it through that one!"

What should Mario have done to solve this problem?

Why was it wrong for Mario to think he "made it through that one?"

Have you ever had trouble solving a problem? What was it?

Is it okay to ask others to help you solve a problem?

Draw a picture of something that presents a problem for you.

Albert takes the same route to and from school every day. Yesterday afternoon, a huge dog confronted him and he was so scared that he ran into a store and called his mom at work. Albert knows that his mom can't take him to school and pick him up every day. What should he do?

What would you do?

Have you ever had a similar problem? What did you do?

23. Attitude

The way you feel about a person or a thing is called your attitude. When you have a good attitude, you are perceived as a pleasant person who is "ready for anything." When you have a negative attitude, people think you're a drag and really don't want to be with you.

The kids in Celia's group were excited about the upcoming project they were assigned to do. Celia thought it was really stupid and decided that even though she had to be at the team meetings, she wasn't going to participate.

Do you think this was right?

____

____

____

Why do you think Celia felt that way?

What could she do to have a better attitude?

Draw a picture of someone with a good attitude.

SECTION IV: SOCIAL SYSTEM

A child's social system is very important in developing a sense of self-esteem. His interactions with family, friends, teachers and other role models all help develop his sense of well-being and his role in the world at large.

24. Forming Loving Attachments

When we form loving attachments, we feel that we are not alone in the world—we have others to lean on, to relate to, to love and to feel love from them.

Jorge had always been a quiet child, and he never wanted to play with the kids in the neighborhood. When he had to go to school for the first time, he was really scared.

What would you have suggested that he could do to make friends?

he

What should Jorge do when other kids try to make friends with him?

What do you do to make new friends?

Draw some things that kids can share.

Lisa was a child whose parents were killed in a car accident. She had been a happy child, but when her parents died she became withdrawn and sad. She went to live with her aunt and cousins. No matter what they did, Lisa wouldn't "open up and let them in." Why do you think Lisa felt this way?

____

____

____

What would you say to Lisa?

____

____

____

Have you ever felt that life was very cruel to you? Write a few lines about it.

____

____

____

25. The Family

How you perceive your family life and your interactions with family members molds and remolds your sense of self and your sense of yourself in the world. If you are nurtured by your parents and feel love from them and your siblings, you'll be much better equipped to face the ups and downs of life than if your family life is unstable.

Gary never knew that his family was weird until he invited Skip over to play. The next day, he heard Skip telling the other kids about the mess in his house and the way his mother dressed. He felt embarrassed and ashamed, and he didn't know what to do about his feelings.

What would you say to him?

"It's okay people have different way of doing things in there house."

Has anything like this ever happened to you? What did you do?

I don't know if any thing like this every happend.

Draw Gary at home and at school.

Paul was always looking for excuses so that he didn't have to go right home after school. The other kids thought it was because he liked to have fun, but it was really because his father was an alcoholic who didn't have a job — and Paul was afraid his dad would hit him.

Why do you think he felt this way?

Is there anything he could say to his dad? What advice would you give him?

Susan looked forward to Mother's Day because she'd have a chance to see her relatives and to play with her cousins. She liked family gatherings because it was fun to be with her relatives.

Why do you think she felt this way?

How do you feel at family gatherings? Why do you feel that way?

Draw a family gathering.

26. Peer Groups

A peer group is the group of people to which you "belong" and with whom you feel comfortable. Your peers can influence how you feel about certain things and what you do. Often, people "go along with" their peers in order to "fit in." Most of the time, this is okay, but sometimes, when a group of people is doing something that is not socially acceptable, it is best not to join your peers.

Salvatore felt really good when Joe asked him to hang at the park with him and the "cool" kids. When they got to the park, the group decided to play basketball. Sal didn't want to play, and told everyone that if they didn't do what he wanted, he'd leave.

Do you think Sal was right to do this?

What should he have done instead?

Fred knew that Sam and Ted were into drugs, but they also had the most awesome card collections and he really wanted to see them. He didn't know what to do—if he went with them after school, he knew they'd try to make him smoke a joint with them, and he didn't want to. What should he have done?

What could he have said to Sam and Ted to assert himself?

Donna really wanted the Tame Flames tape, but she didn't have enough money to pay for it. It would fit into her pocket so easily...but she knew that Sally and Heather would think she was wrong for taking it. She left the store with her pockets empty. Why do you think she didn't steal the tape?

Do you think what Donna did was right or wrong? Why?

27. Extended Family/Community Relationships

Our "extended family" doesn't just refer to our cousins and aunts and uncles. Extended family can include friends, neighbors — anyone to whom you feel close.

As she was on her way to Sarita's house, Tamara's next-door neighbor Mrs. Hughes asked Tamara to help her in the garden. "I don't feel like doing this," thought Tamara, but she put her stuff down and helped Mrs. Hughes anyway.

Why do you think Tamara did this?

What would you have done?

Why is it important to help others?

When you help someone, is there anything "in it" for you?

Draw Tamara helping someone else in a different situation.

28. Dealing with New Situations

Learning to be comfortable in new situations is a social skill that can help you wherever you go...for your whole life.

Kyle's parents wanted him to join the baseball team at the community center. "But I don't know anyone," he complained. "You'll meet new people," his dad said. But Kyle felt scared and nervous.

Why do you think he felt this way?

What could he do or say to feel less nervous?

What would you do in this situation?

Randy was a kid who felt left out all the time. When he moved to a new neighborhood he decided that the only way to get people to notice him was to become a bully. He thought, "People will definitely notice me now!" Was he right to do this?

____

____

____

How would you handle moving to a new neighborhood?

____

____

____

Has anything like this ever happened to you?

____

____

____

Draw Randy in his new neighborhood.